To the Reader…

Our purpose in creating this series is to provide young readers with accurate accounts of the lives of Native American men and women important in the history of their tribes. The stories are written by scholars, including American Indians.

Native Americans are as much a part of North American life today as they were one hundred years ago. Even in times past, Indians were not all the same. Not all of them lived in teepees or wore feather warbonnets. They were not all warriors. Some did fight against the white man, but many befriended him.

Whether patriot or politician, athlete or artist, Arapaho or Zuni, the story of each person in this series deserves to be told. Whether the individuals gained distinction on the battlefield or the playing field, in the courtroom or the classroom, they have enriched the heritage and history of all Americans. It is hoped that those who read their stories will realize that many different peoples, regardless of culture or color, have played a part in shaping the United States and Canada, in making both countries what they are today.

Herman J. Viola
General Editor
Author of *Exploring the West*
and other volumes on the West
and Native Americans

GENERAL EDITOR
Herman J. Viola
Author of *Exploring the West* and other volumes on the West
and American Indians

MANAGING EDITOR
Robert M. Kvasnicka
Coeditor of *The Commissioners of Indian Affairs, 1824–1977*
Coeditor of *Indian-White Relations: A Persistent Paradox*

MANUSCRIPT EDITOR
Barbara J. Behm

DESIGNER
Kathleen A. Hartnett

PRODUCTION
Andrew Rupniewski
Eileen Rickey

First Steck-Vaughn Edition 1992

Library of Congress Number: 89-10533

    4 5 6 7 8 9   97 96 95 94 93 92

Library of Congress Cataloging-in-Publication Data

Morrow, Mary Frances.
  Sarah Winnemucca.
  (Raintree American Indian stories)
  Summary: Recounts the life story of the influential Paiute woman
who fought for justice and a better life for her people.
  1. Hopkins, Sarah Winnemucca, 1844-1891—Juvenile
literature.   2. Paiute Indians—Biography—Juvenile literature.
3. Scouts and scouting—California—Biography—Juvenile
literature.   4. Scouts and scouting—Nevada—Biography—Juvenile
literature.   5. California—Biography—Juvenile literature.
6. Nevada—Biography—Juvenile literature.   [1. Hopkins, Sarah
Winnemucca, 1844-1891.   2. Paiute Indians—Biography.
3. Indians of North America—Biography]   I. Title.   II. Series.
E99.P2H726   1989   979'.00497402   [B]   [92]   89-10533
ISBN 0-8172-3402-0   hardcover library binding
ISBN 0-8114-4095-8   softcover binding

SARAH WINNEMUCCA

Text by Mary Frances Morrow
Illustrations by Ken Bronikowski

A RIVILO BOOK

RSVP

RAINTREE
STECK-VAUGHN
PUBLISHERS
The Steck-Vaughn Company

Sarah Winnemucca was a courageous full-blood Paiute Indian who became a well-known spokesperson for Indian rights. This was quite an achievement in a time when few women or Indians became leaders. White people called her Princess Sarah, a title she liked because it created interest in her and therefore her causes. Her Indian name was *Thoc-me-tony,* which means "Shell

Flower." She chose the name *Sarah* when she grew up. Sarah's father was Chief Winnemucca. Her grandfather, who was known as Captain Truckee, and her brothers also were leaders of their band of Northern Paiutes.

Sarah was born in 1844 in what is today the state of Nevada. Before she was born, very few white people had seen the lakes and mountains of her homeland. Sometimes an occasional explorer or trapper would pass through the lands of the Northern Paiute.

When Sarah was very young, Captain Truckee befriended the explorer John C. Frémont and went with him to California. Captain Truckee came to respect many things that he learned about white people. He admired their clothing and houses, and he admired their ability to write. When he returned to Nevada, he persuaded some of his people to go back with him to California. Captain Truckee wanted his people to be friends with the whites.

Sarah was afraid of white people when she was little. Paiute children were told that the whites were monsters who would kill them. One day the women of her band heard rumors that white people were in the valley. Sarah's mother and aunt snatched up their little girls and ran to hide in the hills.

The women decided to hide the girls in the ground. They dug a hole and buried Sarah and her cousin so only their faces showed. Then they covered the children's faces with bushes.

They warned the little girls not to reveal their hiding places by crying. The two girls lay in the ground all day, hearts throbbing, hardly daring to breathe. When it was dark, their mothers came for them. Sarah was so frightened by that terrible experience that for many years she would tremble and burst into tears whenever she thought of it.

Sarah's home was a wigwam constructed of branches and brush, which was sometimes covered with hides or bark. The people wore clothing made of skins or twisted strips of rabbit fur and wild plant materials. Food was not plentiful, and people often went hungry. Their lives depended upon their being able to move around to find food. Large game such as antelope, deer, and mountain sheep were already in short supply. The men caught fish and hunted rabbits. Fish and meat were preserved by drying them in the sun and wind. The women gathered seeds and ground them between big round stones to prepare them for cooking. When summer came, several families moved together to the mountains where they gathered pine nuts and stored them for use during the following winter.

Sarah grew up surrounded by the interesting sights, sounds, and customs of her people. One especially fascinating person in the Winnemucca band was the medicine man. He communicated with the sacred spirits in a place called Spirit Land. Sarah remembered a message that the medicine man once received. It was "Our people will not all die at the hands of our white brothers. They will kill a great many of us with their guns, but they will bring among us a fearful disease that will cause us to die by the hundreds."

The Paiutes participated in many sacred ceremonies which intrigued young Sarah. The antelope charm ceremony was conducted by her father. It was done to attract antelope that were needed to feed the Paiutes. First, Chief Winnemucca would have his people mark out a large circle on the ground with six mounds of sagebrush and stones. Every morning and every evening the people would sit around an opening in the circle, smoking a special pipe and passing it around the circle five times to the right. The Northern Paiutes also had a special musical instrument, a drum, that was played only in the antelope charm ceremony. Sarah's father rubbed the drum with a stick to make an eerie, vibrating sound. He then led the people in singing antelope charm songs.

Each day for five days, two men carrying torches would run in opposite directions around a herd of antelope. The people followed the torchbearers but did not let the antelope see them. On the fifth day, the charm was complete, and the antelope would follow the people into the circle of brush and stay there just as if a fence enclosed them.

Captain Truckee eventually returned from California. He sat by the fire for days and talked about the white people. He said whites were their brothers and were kind to everybody, especially children. He told about their ships that looked like houses on water. He sang the "Star Spangled Banner" to his people. He showed all his people a paper with writing on it that he called his "rag friend." He said, "This can talk to all our white brothers, and our white sisters, and their children." He said it could travel like the wind. It could go and talk to white families and come back and tell what they were doing. Sarah was very impressed with her grandfather's stories about the writings of white people.

Sarah and her mother went with Captain Truckee on his next trip to California. On the journey, Sarah met white people for the first time. Once she became very sick with poison oak. Her face swelled up so badly that she could not see. A kind white woman put medicine on her face and talked to her. As Sarah got better, the lady visited her and brought gifts—sweet things to eat and pretty dresses. Sarah began to lose her fear of whites.

When Sarah and her family returned to Nevada, they found that many of their people had died from disease, just as the medicine man had predicted. The women cut off their hair to mourn the dead. The men told her grandfather that the people had died after drinking the water. They thought white people had poisoned the river. Captain Truckee pointed out that if the whites had poisoned the water, it would also have poisoned the white people when they drank it. He said the sickness was some new, dreadful disease.

Years later in 1858, when Sarah was about fourteen, she and her sister had the opportunity to live with the family of a white settler, Major William Ormsby. They lived there for a year, taking care of his little daughter. They learned very quickly to speak English.

As more white people moved into the area, hostilities began between the Paiutes and the settlers. When two white men were killed, the Indians were mistakenly blamed. In retaliation, whites shot and killed three Indians.

Not long after that incident, Sarah's grandfather died. His last wish was for Sarah and her sister to attend a mission school in California. They were at the mission school only three weeks when parents of white children complained about their children having to associate with Indians. For that reason, Sarah and her sister were forced to leave. Even though Sarah did not receive a great deal of formal schooling, she learned to speak English, Spanish, and two Indian languages. She learned to read and write, and in 1883 she coauthored a book called *Life Among the Paiutes: Their Claims and Wrongs.*

In 1860, Major Ormsby was killed in a war between the Indians and whites. A truce was declared and Sarah's people were forced to settle on the Pyramid Lake Reservation. At first only Paiutes lived on the Indian land, but after a railroad was cut through in 1867, whites moved in. When the whites took the best land and a lake from the Indians, trouble began. Indians were accused of stealing cattle, and soldiers hunted down the Indians and killed many of them.

The government appointed an agent to be in charge of the reservation Indians. He was supposed to issue food and clothing to the Indians, but they never received enough supplies. The Indians accused the agent of holding back the goods in order to sell them and get rich himself. Since Sarah could speak English and Indian languages, she often served as an interpreter. The Indians asked her to tell the government that they were not receiving their supplies.

Sarah went to see General John Schofield in San Francisco. She told him her people were not given seeds to plant for crops and were not shown how to farm, although they were expected to raise their own food. She said the teachers in the school did not teach the children to read and write or to speak English. She said they had no lumber for houses, no ammunition to hunt for game, and no material for clothing. The Indians had been told that the land was not really theirs and that they had to pay for its use. She said the agents lied to reporters, telling them about buildings and bridges that were supposedly there but were never really built.

The general advised Sarah to contact Senator John P. Jones at Gold Hill, Nevada. Senator Jones listened to Sarah and gave her a gold piece, but he did nothing else to help her people.

In 1875, Sarah was asked to serve as an interpreter at the Malheur Reservation in Oregon. This reservation had been set aside in 1867, and it became the Paiutes' new home. The agent, Sam B. Parrish, was a good man who treated the Indian people fairly. He taught them how to dig irrigation ditches for their fields and how to build fences. He set up a school where all the Indian children were taught to read and the young boys were taught to be blacksmiths and carpenters. He helped the Indians plant potatoes, turnips, and watermelons. He gave the people flour, beef, and beans. He gave them ammunition for hunting. He paid the people a fair wage for their work.

The Indians were very happy with Agent Parrish, but then the government decided to change agents. The agent who arrived in 1876 was William V. Rinehart. He had little sympathy for the Indians or their needs. The Indians disliked him intensely, and they disapproved of his policies. Rinehart told them that if they did not like what he was doing, they could leave. The Indians all left the reservation.

Things got worse for the Indians. In June 1878, the Bannocks, a neighboring tribe, went on the warpath. They were starving and unable to support themselves. They persuaded the war chief Egan and some other Paiutes to join them, and these men forced Sarah's father to go on the warpath also.

The captain of the United States Army Cavalry wanted to contact Chief Winnemucca to ask him not to join the hostile Indians, but Sarah's father and others were already being held prisoner by the Bannocks. No one would deliver a message to him because they were afraid to go into the Bannocks' territory. Finally, Sarah agreed to take the message. She followed the Bannocks' trail for many miles. She sneaked into the camp at night, crawling on her hands and knees. She told her father that the army would help him and his people if they would leave the Bannocks.

The women left the camp as if they were searching for firewood. Once they had made their way out of camp, they escaped. Chief Winnemucca told several of the men to get horses. The Bannocks heard the commotion and began chasing the men. Sarah and her father and his people all escaped. A month later, the army defeated the Bannocks and a few Paiutes in battle. The captured Indians were forced onto the Yakima Reservation in the Washington Territory. Even Paiutes who had not fought were made to live on the reservation.

During the winter of 1879-1880, Sarah, her father, her brother, and a few others traveled to Washington, D.C., to meet President Rutherford B. Hayes and Secretary of the Interior Carl Schurz. Schurz was responsible for administering the government's Indian policy. Sarah told him all about the Bannock War. Because only a few Paiutes had joined the fighting, she said it was unfair that so many were separated from their families. She wanted Schurz to remove Agent Rinehart and permit the Paiutes to move to the Malheur Reservation, which they considered home.

Before Sarah left Washington, D.C., Schurz gave her a letter saying that all nonhostile Paiutes could move to the Malheur Reservation if they wanted to. Sarah was very happy and considered her mission a success.

The agent at Yakima refused to let the Paiutes go to the Malheur Reservation because they did not have the money to buy the clothing, horses, and supplies they needed for the trip. He said they would suffer and die without supplies. He also wanted them to wait until soldiers were available to escort them past hostile whites. It was two more years before the Paiutes left Yakima. Because of the long delay, Sarah felt that her efforts had been a failure.

Sarah continued to work for many years for her people. She wanted them to be given land to raise their own crops. She wanted the children to learn English and to read and write. But she did not want them to lose their tribal identity or to forget their pride in being Indians.

Sarah worked as an interpreter, guide, and scout for various government officials. She also taught school and went on trips to the East to lecture to groups of white people. She told them what was happening on the Indian reservations. In her lectures, Sarah told her audiences that Paiute Indians let everyone express their opinions during councils. She said that women knew as much about tribal affairs as men did and often gave their advice. She said, "If women could go into your Congress, I think justice would be done to the Indians."

While on a lecture tour, Sarah met Elizabeth Peabody and her sister, Mary Peabody Mann, the wife of the educational reformer, Horace Mann. These women became her staunch supporters. Both sisters encouraged her and raised money to help educate her people. Sarah called the school that was built with the funds the Peabody School.

Sarah was an unusual woman, accomplished in languages and skilled as a speaker. She was courageous in her willingness to speak out against injustice. She tried to call attention to the ways in which her people had been wronged. She tried to help her people by speaking out for them and by teaching the children to speak for themselves. Sarah Winnemucca died in 1891 at the age of forty-seven. In her short life, she won a place in history as one of America's most honored Indian women.

HISTORY OF SARAH WINNEMUCCA

1844	Sarah Winnemucca was born.
1848	Gold was discovered in California. The Treaty of Guadalupe Hidalgo ended the war with Mexico.
1860	The pony express began.
1861-1865	The Civil War was fought. Abraham Lincoln was president.
1864	Camels were used as pack animals in Nevada Territory.
1860s & 1870s	Sarah Winnemucca served as an interpreter, guide, and scout for various government officials.
1867	A railroad was built through Paiute land on the Pyramid Lake reserve, and white people began moving in.
1870	Sarah Winnemucca began to speak out about the government's mistreatment of her people.
1880	Sarah Winnemucca met with President Rutherford B. Hayes to discuss the plight of her people. Sarah's father, Chief Winnemucca, died.
1881	Sarah Winnemucca opened a school in Washington Territory for Indian children.
1883	Sarah Winnemucca coauthored a book called *Life Among the Paiutes: Their Claims and Wrongs*.
1888	Wovoka, a Paiute Indian, began preaching his Ghost Dance religion.
1890	Sioux participation in the Ghost Dance led to the Battle of Wounded Knee (South Dakota).
1891	Sarah Winnemucca died.